Improve Career in Software

Dedicated to my son Ayaan

Author information

For any help please contact :
Amazon Author Page :
amazon.com/author/ajaykumar
Email : ajaycucek@gmail.com ,
ajaxreso@gmail.com
Linkedin :
https://www.linkedin.com/in/ajaycucek
Facebook :
https://www.facebook.com/ajaycucek
Youtube :
https://www.youtube.com/channel/UC1uXE
ebtqCLYxVdzirKZGIA
Twitter : https://twitter.com/ajaycucek
Instagram :
https://www.instagram.com/ajaycucek/
Skype : ajaycucek

Table of contents

Module 1 : Introduction

Introduction

This book is about improving Career in Software. This book is the result of years of experience in the software industry. During that time I've held a variety of roles from software development and management to developer evangelism, developer marketing, customer feedback, and influencer programs. It's been an interesting journey that has allowed me to speak with thousands and thousands of developers from a variety of angles. Along the way I've seen some interesting patterns emerge that distinctly identify successful developers and are clearly missing from less successful developers. It's something I've wanted to formally capture for a long time as I've not seen it pulled together anywhere else. I'm going to share with you five patterns, or principles, that I've seen over and over in more successful developers that I've met with over the years. There may be other principles, and some of these may be more important for you to learn than others. It's not intended to be an exhaustive list, but rather a helpful set of principles you ought to consider if you are a software developer. All of the items on this list are fairly easy to implement and I've included some tangible ways to do each of the principles. I hope that you'll find the information useful and that perhaps something in this book could serve as a catalyst to help you have a more successful career in software.

Agenda

Core principles for a better career in software :

- Technology - Becoming an expertise expert
- Growth - Managing your career
- Framing - Solving problems in context
- Brand - Taking care of your reputation
- Interactions - Working and playing well with others

Let's take a look at what we're going to cover. I've grouped these loosely into the buckets you see on the slide. The lines between the categories are not clean and distinct, but I think that accurately represents reality as these topics have some overlap in places. The five areas we'll discuss are, number one, becoming an expertise expert. You could subtitle this one, marry your career, date your technology. Number two, managing your career. This is really about you owning your career path. Number three, solving problems with proper context, you need to understand why you do what you do. Number four, taking care of your reputation. You are ultimately limited by how others perceive you. Number five, work and play well with others. Basically this says, don't be that guy. We'll talk about what each of these principles really mean and get some tactical guidance on how to implement each of them in your work. And with that, let's dive right into the first item, which is the principle of becoming an expert in technology itself.

Module 2 : Technology

Introduction

Technology Awareness
- Are you an expert in something that matters?
- Three things people do that hurt their careers
  - 1) pick a fringe technology
  - 2) cling to a fading technology
  - 3) hold an emotional attachment to a technology

The first area I want to cover is technology awareness. You may not realize it, but you are an expert in something; you almost can't not be an expert in something. You spend your time during the day in some capacity, and over time you are naturally going to get good at whatever that thing is. It may just be the details of business at your job, it may be a programming language, it could be your infrastructure, but you're good at something. The question is, with apologies for ending in a preposition, what are you actually good at? Generally speaking, there are three ways people tend to hurt their careers when it comes to their expertise. Number one, they attach themselves to a technology without paying attention to its popularity or relevance in the industry. Number two, and it's related to the first item, they hang on to a technology they know, ignoring its age or the way it is trending in the industry. And number three, they move away from technical merit and instead they make emotional decisions as opposed to intellectual decisions around which technology to choose for a given problem. We'll take a deeper look at each of these three areas and how they can help or hurt your career in software.

Relevance

The Relevance of a Technology
- Does what you know –matter?
Okay, let me start by asking two questions here, what technology would you say you are most proficient in today? Second, why are you proficient in that? The second question

can be very revealing, it's easy to simply use whatever your company has you working with day to day. And it might be an ideal choice, but for many developers they are simply letting their skill set emerge as a result of the company's decisions. Or worse yet, they're locked in on some fringe technology that they think is cool, but very few others are using. This talk is around having a better career in software and one of the first things you need to understand here is that you need to have a marketable skill. There are plenty of mainstream technologies, like. NET, Java, C, and others. You don't have to pick one of those, but it might be smart to go to a site like CareerBuilder and do a search on your primary expertise to see who else is using it. You want to be good at things that other people are using, that is the essence of marketability, having a skill set that is in demand. When was the last time you looked at your skills and compared them to what's in demand today? If you're not getting any calls from recruiters, it might be because you're doing something no one cares about. Don't blow past this too quickly, if you want to have a better career in software, a key component is having a skill that people care about. In the second section of this book, I'll talk about how to expand your skill set, but for now I challenge you to honestly look at what you can offer a company, and perhaps start to think about the skill set you'd like to have. Sometimes people ask me what skills are the best ones to have. And while there's not a clear answer, I often tell developers to look at session topics of major conferences. Companies like Microsoft and Google typically telegraph their emerging technology areas in their session topics at major conferences. If you're looking for something new to learn, look at what they're talking about, and you'll at least have an idea of the things they will be focused on in the coming year. There are many websites, such as TOB. com, that track language usage. It's smart to know where your current tooling and technology usage stands on sites like this. Note that there are solutions where a fringe skill set carries a very high bill rate, so it's not just a matter of taking the broadest technology and running with it, but recognize that generally speaking, the narrower a skill is that you have, the fewer options you'll have with it. It's also great to see what search terms are popular on the job boards. If you're doing something that is not showing up in conferences and not showing up on job boards, I'd suggest doing something else. Or at least adding a new, more in-demand skill, to your arsenal.

Clinging

Let's talk about clinging to a declining technology. This is really a specific case of the item we just mentioned, but it is so common that I think it merits its own mention. There is nothing wrong with picking and staying with a technology for several years, however, you need to be intentional about it rather than just doing it because you're still getting a paycheck for it. Programmers tend to have an affinity for the things they know, it's in our DNA to like what we use and to push back on what we don't use. That's a default setting for us, but smart developers will recognize it and will track where a specific technology is with respect to its window of relevance. You see every technology has a window during which it matters. Some technologies are very long lived, C and C++ for example are actually seeing an uptake in relevance and have been relevant for 15+ years. Other technologies, like the ironically named Flash, sprang up quickly and looked to be centrally positioned only to have HTML5 and JavaScript assume much of the value they initially offered. Will Flash die out? I don't know. But certainly C and C++ have carried a longer and more steady window of market share. Referring back to the websites like TOB, if you're using a technology and sites like this show it decaying in usage, you need to recognize that and you need to think about picking up a skill that offers more opportunity down the road. It's impossible to predict exactly what's going to happen in our industry, but successful developers are on a continuous learning journey, and recognizing when to update your skill set is a core component of a successful career in software.

Taking Stands

I can't tell you how many companies I've been in where I've heard an almost identical refrain from the people whose primary role is supposed to be technical adviser to the leadership. And it is stunning that someone who is supposed to be knowing and recommending technologies would do this, but I see it all the time. I see people declaring a standard that is clearly based on some stupid religious stand, and yes I said stupid, no one technology is perfect for every situation. In my arena, I see huge enterprises throwing out a blanket decree like, we'll do all our development in Java, or. NET, or whatever. Whenever I hear this I know one thing for certain, somewhere behind the scenes is someone taking a religious stand over a technology, and it's almost certainly based on what they've used in the past rather than what is the best technology for the situation. Understand, I am not saying you should avoid standards. Standards are good and helpful, and if you have centralized development it may make sense to pick one thing and go with it. But that is rarely, actually in my experience, never, the case. In almost every situation I've ever seen, and I've seen a ton of them, whatever the architect and the decision making authority likes is decreed upon the entire body of developers and is generally dished out with great emotional energy. If you hear anyone in a technical decision-making role using words like hate, sucks, crap, and other emotive terms, that's almost always an unhealthy sign. To make their case, generally they're comparing a current or future version of the product they love with a 5 or 10 year old version of the other technology, which is probably the last time they actually looked at it. This is dangerous, but all too common. I see more energy wasted on religious technology decisions than almost any other thing in enterprises. These kind of decrees never last, they usually change shortly after the person who decreed them moves on, or you have factions pop up and little fiefdoms that create all kinds of sideways energy and integration problems. How do you solve it? It's not easy. For starters, any standards body should have representation for all relevant technologies, and they should explicitly watch for, and call out emotional versus technical decision making, and then come to agreement from there. Will that work? I can't say for sure, but I can say that taking a religious stand on technology almost never works long term and eventually creates more work than just letting people do what they want. If you want to have a better career in software, don't allow yourself to fall into the trap of crusading for a technology simply because you like it. That will almost always never end well.

Summary

Becoming an Expertise Expert
- Technology awareness
  - Check its relevance
  - Check its age/momentum
  - Use information, not emotion, when choosing it

The bottom line here is, any specific technology is a temporary thing. It has a window of relevance, and when that's over, you need to learn something new. As developers we tend to emotionally attach to our current technology and defend it in all situations regardless of its appropriateness or fit in the business situation at hand.

Successful developers can look beyond their innate attachment to a technology, and are mindful about when to use it, as well as when to move to a new technology. Separating technology from your personal affinities is a huge point of growth, which is why we listed it as the first of our five principles for a better career in software.

Module 3 : Personal Growth

Introduction

Managing Your Career
- **You own your career**
    - **Natural strengths**
    - **Career planning**
    - **Course correcting**
    - **Learning styles**
    - **Job hopping**

Now let's talk about Managing Your Career. When it comes to an awareness of your career path, a lot of the things I want to cover are common sense. You may nod your head in agreement as you hear them and say you already know that. I've suggested many of these things to developers over the years and they often say, yes I already know that, already know that, but they are typically not doing it. As Patrick Lencioni has said, most of the great truths in life we already know, we simply need to be reminded of them. So with that in mind, I'll go through these and propose that even if you hear and recognize them, take a little time to think through whether you are actually doing them or not. It's been said that unapplied knowledge is like unapplied paint, it doesn't make things any better. All of these things fall under a general truth about managing your career path, and this is a central truth, you own your career. Other people can make things harder or easier, jobs may come and go, and technologies may come and go as well, but the bottom line is, at the end of the day, you own your career. Life is not always fair and you can't count on other people to take care of you. It is on you to take steps to make yourself valuable to your employer. With that as the backdrop, here are the five things I suggest to people when it comes to managing their career paths. Number one, know what you're actually good at. What are you a natural at doing? Know where you want to be in five years. What are you trying to become? Number three, check where you are along the way and are you making progress towards those goals? Number four, take an intentional instead of a reactive learning approach. Do you have a road map for the next thing you want to be or do? And number five, don't jump around from job to job just for the sake of a small raise or because you got mad at someone. We'll take a look at each of these five items next.

Strengths

This one is really easy to figure out, although I think the majority of people never take time to explicitly discover it for themselves. Whenever I'm in a corporate meeting with a large team, or at a conference, I love to people watch because it reveals so much about them. Many of the conferences I attend have a platform for the speakers and rows of tables for the attendees to put their computers, slates, notebooks, whatever on, along with a pen and a pad for each attendee. And that pen and pad are incredibly revealing. Some attendees will listen intently taking clean, bulleted notes as we go. Others will doodle in the margins while they listen. Still others can't help themselves, they take the pens apart and usually end up ruining them. Still others will stack the pads and use coffee creamers as foundations with sugar packets and flatware and construct their own little metropolis while I desperately try to hold their attention. And finally, some will ignore all the materials on the table and would rather sit there and fact check everything I say, searching the web to see if they can disprove whatever I am showing them. Now, it's way oversimplified to say it this way, but here goes, the bulleted note takers are probably your project managers, the doodlers are probably your designers, the pen disassemblers are likely your engineers, and the city builders are your architects, and the fact checkers are your testers. Now I know, I know that's generalizing everybody and short selling them. Some of it probably depends on how much sugar and caffeine they've had on that day, but my point is people are naturally different in what they are drawn to. I used to work with a guy who we made attend meetings initially, and the poor guy couldn't last 5 minutes before he had his pen in pieces, several pages torn out of his notepad, and he was drumming the pen parts on the table distracting everyone. He was miserable in meetings and he really had nothing to contribute there, but I could give him some crazy bug and he would go find it and fix it faster than anyone else on the team. I told our CTO to quit putting the poor guy in meetings and everyone was so much happier that way. We put him back in a corner and gave him these really hard problems and he was great, he solved problems that no one else could touch. It was simply a matter of aligning him to his natural strengths. People are just naturally better at certain things. I believe we are innately created that way. Surfacing your natural strengths is key to having a better career in software. One other quote, Albert Einstein said, if you judge a fish by its ability to climb a tree, it will live its whole life believing that it is stupid. Do you know what you're best at doing? If you do a lot of different things at your job, which ones do you enjoy? Which ones give you the most enjoyment and energy? There is probably something that you do, and when you're doing it the day flies by. There are probably other things that you put off doing and you grit your teeth as you pound through it. This should be a tip as to where your natural strengths are. You'll do your best work doing what you love, and that's the point I want to make. If you've never taken the time to learn what you do best, how can you focus on it? I often tell people that I mentor to do their job well and stretch into the areas they enjoy the most. There are cases where you may want to do something and you're just not naturally good at it. I can't help but think of the bad singers on American Idol here. One of my former general managers used to tell us, we want you guys to blog, but don't do it if you suck at it. It was blunt, but what great advice. If you don't like blogging, and you try to do it, you probably won't enjoy it and neither will your readers if you ever have any. Figure out what you like and what you seem to be pretty good at doing, and without neglecting your primary duties at work, expand into that area. If you can't formally do it, then learn about that area and get better at it. If you were to rank your abilities on a scale of 1 to 10, and you're naturally a 4 out of 10 at something, then you probably can train yourself to be a 6, but you're not helping that much. However, if you're naturally an 8 at something, you can train yourself to be a 10 and you'll be much more valuable. And the odds are high that your company will eventually move you into that role that lets you do it. And if not, someone else will eventually come along and recruit you away to do that thing. We'll talk more about how to move from an 8 to a 10 in the next few areas.

Making Plans

I've heard numerous leaders and mentors
say, if you don't know where you want to go,
you probably won't get there. So let me ask
you, do you know what you want to be? And
I don't mean retired on a boat in the South
Pacific, I mean with respect to your career.
If you had a magic wand and could create
the perfect role for yourself what would it
be? This is a valuable exercise to think
through this, and look at what the barriers
are for yourself. What is between you and
that ideal position? If you had things go
exactly as you want, where would you be in
five years? There are many goal setting
books and books out there, I won't advocate
any specific one. I think it's more important
to take 5 minutes and just think about it. As
a matter of fact, I suggest you doing that
now. Pause this book and think about it, and
then continue. Whether or not you did that
just now, it's a valuable thing to do, and it
really doesn't take very long to get an idea of
where you want to go. Once you know that,
what things are between you and that goal?
Is it a matter of just getting some
certifications? Reading some books?
Speaking at a few local events? Maybe
writing an article or a book? What are some
specific tactics that can get you where you
want to be in five years? Once you can name
them, you can start the journey there. I'll
talk about how to learn in the last part of
this section, but it's actually easier than you
think. Everybody tends to see this as a much
tougher thing than it really is. The key point

here is know where you want to go and take a little time to think through how to get there. Until you do that, you're probably going to just meander through your career and end up wherever your manager has pointed you.

Book Correcting

If you've done any Agile programming, you probably know that it can be summed up as continual conversations so that you can book correct. Waterfall development is all about creating a concrete requirement and then setting off to create it. It doesn't really provide a good mechanism to book correct. Agile let's you take a small scoop of things off the backlog, build them, and then evaluate and adjust as needed. Your career will benefit from this same kind of thinking. There have been a few times in my career where I've gone heads down on a project for a good 12 to 18 months, and then when I come up for air there's a whole new wave of technologies that have popped up and I'm already behind. Much like that, you need to always have an eye on where you're going. Have you been plowing away for a few years on the same project? What new things have you learned in the past 12 months? I always find value in looking back over my last 12 months, my last 5 years, and my last 10 years to see how much I've grown and learned. This gives me great view of my trajectory and helps me think about how to spend the next 12 months in my growth areas. I like to ask the question, where was I five years ago?

I you are continual improving yourself this can be very rewarding. And on the contrary, if you are effectively the same place you were five years ago, you're likely not progressing in your career. Now, that may be okay if you're content to coast and if you have the security to do that, but I would highly recommend you taking time to think about what you were doing last year at this time, five years ago at this time, and 10 years ago at this time. Are you progressing, or are you just clicking along doing the same thing day after day? Based on that answer, what do you need to do in the next 12 months to adjust? You should take time, at least once a year, to reflect, project, and book correct. This is another key component to having a better career in software.

Learning

If you can remember back to your college days, there were many times when we learned by cramming for a test. For me, I usually got good grades doing that, but one day later I remembered almost nothing from those late night cram-athons. The process was more like a sponge filling my brain with numbers and facts, and then squeezing them out at test time never to recall them again. That may be an effective way to pass a test, but it's a horrible way to learn a new skill set. If you want to have a better career in software, it's essential to build new skill sets through scheduled, gradual learning. When I wanted to learn COM back in the 90s, I had three books. I kept them by my bed and I read for 20 minutes each night. They were about 300 pages each so I could get about 15 pages in a night. This means that I read a book every three weeks. When I got the end I would just start over again. I read each book multiple times and in about six months I was quite the expert in COM. Had I taken a weekend and gone dark to cut down these books, it would have been very much a short term learning. Also, I found that by taking notes and coding the examples, I could retain a lot more information. This kind of application forced me to make a decision based on what I learned rather than merely drinking it in by reading. What books, articles, books, or webcasts have you taken in the past 12 months? At least there's this book, so clearly you've taken part of at least one. Sometimes I make a goal along the lines of, read one article and one webcast per week. I keep a lot of podcasts on my phone, everything from Harvard Business Review to software books. You'd be surprised how easy it is to get in an hour a week while driving or exercising. I always tell people that instead of watching 3 hours of TV every night, you could watch 2. 5 hours, use the other half hour to study, and totally revamp your career in about a 6 months. That's not a hard proposition, it's a lot better than cramming and way more effective as well. Almost without exception, every successful developer I know is in a state of continual learning. They're not over the top about it, they merely take in a couple of new things each week. Maybe all of 2 hours a week. And regardless what technology is the flavor of the month, they seem to be on top of things.

Job Hopping

The last area I wanted to include in the career paths category is job hopping. I've have a lot of friends that have made a career out of jumping from company to company. They usually get a menial raise and enjoy changing the scenery. They also seem to remain, ultimately, at a fairly flat level as the small raises are eventually offset by a step down. No matter what company you work for, even if you're independent, there are non-technical aspects of the job that add value. You generally reset those when you change jobs. For example, if you're coding in the healthcare industry, there are all kinds of rules and regulations you need to know, and they show up in your algorithms, they impact your testing, they often drive your requirements. If you jump to another company in the same industry, that knowledge is probably not useful in the new role. Now I'm not saying you should find a company and work there for 30 years, but I am saying that the longer you stay with the company, the more of that metadata you'll pick up, which will make you more valuable to that company. Most people job hop because they get mad or because they get an offer that's a nominal raise. That's usually a short term win, but the offset of the other knowledge usually cancels it out over time. It's fine to take a new job, especially if it advances your career, like better aligning to what you want to do. But bouncing around every year is going to leave you mostly flat and will likely become a red flag on your resume. At the very least stay around long enough to solve a big problem and then try to leave on good terms. You never know when a former manager will show up at another company down the road. Burnt bridges are hard to cross, this industry appears huge, but the reality is if you remain in the same geographical area, you almost certainly will cross paths with old coworkers along the way. Hopping around introduces some risk with bumping into old coworkers. Be careful about job hopping, and only do so when it is a distinct advantage for you, one that outweighs restarting, and one that outweighs the perceived instability of jumping around.

Summary

Managing Your Career
- Own your career
  - Know your natural strengths
  - Plan your career path
  - Evaluate and course correct along the way
  - Learn proactively, not reactively
  - Be careful about job hopping

The bottom line here is this, you own your career. You may get breaks, both good and bad along the way, but in the end your career is your responsibility. You should know what you're good at doing, you should have a plan to get where you want to go, you should study continually, and you should not bounce all over the place in terms of where you work. All of these will contribute to a better software career.

Module 4 : Framing

Introduction

Solving Problems in Context
- Understanding the larger mission
  - Knowing your company's context
  - The danger of focusing on short term only
  - The danger of focusing on long term only
  - Programming politics
  - Corporate systems
  - Dwelling on the negatives
  - Taking glamorous stands

Now let's turn the page and talk about solving problems in a larger context, specifically, the context of your company. And oh boy, there are so many ways people sabotage their careers when it comes to their company. I have seven of them listed here, but I'm sure there are more. Companies, especially larger ones, are almost always slower moving than individuals, and they become easy targets because of that. People talk in frustrated terms about how companies are slow and clueless, and neither is exactly true. Companies are run by systems, those systems are built and operated by humans, the moving parts are always a bit clunky, some more so than others. Learning how to see this without obsessing over it or going off on it is key to having a better career in software. The seven areas I'll cover around this are, number one, knowing your business context. In other words the real reason why you do what you do. Number two, the danger of focusing on short term only. This is all tactics, no strategy, having your head right against the work. Number three is the danger of focusing on long term only, and that's all strategy, no tactics, and you're not getting anything done. Number four is programming politics, you're going to be working with humans, humans are imperfect, and politics are a part of any organization. Number five is those corporate systems, you'll be working with imperfect systems in addition the imperfect humans. Number six is dwelling on the negatives. You're going to see the things that you look for, whether you're looking for positives or negatives. And number seven, which seems a little bit out on the edge, is taking glamorous stands. The idea here is not to stand out as a contrarian. We'll go into each of these seven areas in this section.

Company

There is a reason your company has an IT Department, I'm being serious here. There is a reason your company developers on staff, and it's not because they love software. If you are consulting, there is a reason why someone is paying you to write code. If you are off building apps on your own, you probably already know this. We may have chosen software development as a career because we enjoy it, but companies are not paying us to write code because they enjoy code, you are being paid to build solutions because your company needs the solution to do its business. You may internal to the company or you may be building a product your company sells. Regardless, you are being paid to create solutions to solve some business problem. One mistake I often see developers make is they forget why they're being paid. It's easy to get lost in your code and miss the bigger context for what you are doing, but that is also detrimental to your career. There will likely be times that you will find yourself in the presence of some bigwig at your company, and I can assure you that person knows exactly why you're being paid. Showing that you understand the business context of your project is a huge plus in the eyes of your management. I'm not talking about kissing up to them, I mean actually figuring out why you're being paid to write code. When that becomes clear, you may find yourself seeing new ways to solve problems and proposing better solutions to your management. A simple way to learn this is to ask, why are you doing it? Ask yourself what value your project brings to the company. Seeing your business context will generally set you up for more success and is a critical component of managing your career path.

Short-sightedness

As much as business context will help you, there's also something to be said around how your work fits into the larger architectural backbone of you company. This is a similar concept to business context, but it is very different in detail. Successful developers pay attention to more than just assigned tasks they are given. They view them in terms of the broader solution. I'm referring to things like buildings APIs that are broadly consumable, including extensibility hooks and pluggability at the right places. And I'm also referring to building a solution that's maintainable, not merely shippable. In terms of consumable, extensible, and pluggable, you may have an idea of how your solution will be used, but it's very hard to predict what is going to happen after you put it into the hands of your customers. As an example, way back in 1990 Visual Basic added the VBX extensibility almost as an afterthought, and an entire cottage industry sprang up around the concept. Simply put, you can't precisely know how your app is going to be used once it's out in the wild, but you can design for extensibility and improve the chances that you'll be able to more easily adapt to the live usage. The second area around short term thinking is the whole short-sided idea of getting something out the door. Technically you can usually ship something more quickly by hard coding parts and other such shortcuts, but that comes at a cost of maintainability. You can also ship more quickly by minimizing testing and letting your customers find the bugs for you. This is very dangerous and very expensive, but it is all too common as teams try to shove software out the door ahead of some artificial deadline. The more successful developers I meet generally think in terms of futures not merely completing the tasks in front of them. As with business context, longer term thinking is a way to show your management that you are both strategic and tactical in your problem solving.

Getting Things Done

With what we've said about understanding full business and architectural context, it's important to say that you do need short term progress and an awareness of your tactical approach. One thing I've seen in many companies where the developers are given freedom, is a team that continually reengineers a product, always creating, but never getting anything out the door. Some of the smartest developer teams I've met are guilty of this continual churn as they think of better and better ways to do something. Continuous innovation is a good thing and continuous improvement is as well, but you need to operate with a sense of progress and with some shippable builds along the way. If you can balance your steady progress with well-placed extensibility points, you are well on your way to a better career in software.

Programming Politics

Now let's turn our attention to a less technical, but absolutely critical matter. I'm going to touch on a few soft skill areas, and most of it can be summed up in simply not having a bad attitude, but we'll look at a couple specific areas to drive home this point. First, if your company employs humans there are going to be politics. I've never worked anywhere, nor have I ever been to a company that was completely free of politicking. It is human nature to have positioning, competitiveness, executive flattery, and power games. And one huge point of growth for a developer is to learn how to navigate politics without becoming immersed in it. Too often I see good programmers get caught up in some political games, and rather than step back, they actually double down on the situation. One of my favorite managers once told me, this is not a hill to dies on. I don't even remember what the issue was, but her saying really stuck with me because as developers we are paid to write code. Ninety percent of the politics in an office have more to do with people than writing code. It is very easy to get involved, but doing so is a surefire way to create barriers, and those barriers may come back to limit your career when you least expect it. The advice here is simple, not everything that can be said should be said. You will have opportunities to get in the middle of all kinds of politics, and doing so will eventually impact your career, likely in a negative fashion.

Systems

As with inner office politics, you are almost guaranteed to interact with large, bulky corporate systems as you build solutions. In some cases you'll actually have to code against them, in other cases it will be something you have to deal with as part of the job, like a bulky timecard software, or a required HR training video. These are easy targets for ridicule, they usually feel clumsy, they have tons of fields that no one uses, or that everyone uses inconsistently, and they tend to be slow and dated. Of course you could make fun of them, but since we've talked about hills to die on, I would suggest this is another area where you limit your commentary. I've had to deal with a lot of these large systems, including as an owner. In one of my more recent cases, there was only one developer left who even understood the system, and he wanted to get out any way he could. The system was full of problems, hard to use, it lost data, and it was barely functional, but it sat at the hub of our large division and I was tasked with keeping it alive without getting any additional resources to do that. My customers complained about the system non-stop, and they had good reason to do so. But the business reality is, we did not have the resources to fix the system at that time. Chances are the people who maintain large systems you use are not idiots, rather large companies focus on large problems and sometimes a system that works poorly, but still works, is good enough for another fiscal year. You have two real choices in this kind of situation, you can either loudly complain about the system, or just grit your teeth and deal with it and get back to your primary job as quickly as possible. My experience is that people who loudly complain about things like this usually are not seeing the same level of success as those who just use the system and move on. Actually, when it comes to some of our internal systems where I work now, such as our HR compliance videos, I've found that taking the books as early as possible actually results in positive visibility. No one says you have to do this, I'm simply pointing out the patterns I see in more successful developers. They understand when there's time to show deference rather than provide needless commentary at every opportunity.

Negativity

Dwelling on the negatives is a more generic aspect of what we've already covered, but it needs to be called out briefly. Outside of politics in big corporate systems there are other opportunities at every company to focus on the negatives. Developers are problem solvers by nature and we often look for problems and call them out, particularly when there is an obvious issue in front of us. Simply put, the more negative you are in those situations, the less likely you are to rise to the top of your team. Negativity breeds negativity, and many managers will actively monitor who is the source of the negativity. You don't want to be pinned with that label. There is a story of two people who drove across America in a car. One of them talked at length about the beautiful mountains, rivers, valleys, and trees. The other one talked about all the trash on the side of the road. Now, they were both right and they both took the same trip, but each one saw what he was looking for. You tend to see what you look for. If you actively look for negative things you will find them. My experience is that the more successful developers don't do that. And it's not that they act all Pollyannaish about things, it's just that some things don't need to be said or dwelt on. Focus on the more positive aspects of your job and you'll be happier, and ultimately more successful.

Random Stands

The final thing I wanted to bring up around working in tandem with your company rather than against it, and I had a hard time finding the right term for this, but it's taking glamorous stands. I'm still not sure that's the best way to put it, but what I mean by this is you don't want to be the company diva, regardless of the topic. Some developers limit their growth simply because they love to debate. You've probably been in a room setting up for a meeting and someone walks in, and as soon as they walk in you groan on the inside because he or she is going to be there. And you know that whatever you talk about this person is going to argue, push back, complain, or in some way slow the meeting down. You don't want to be that person. Also, make sure you hear what I am not saying; I am not saying that you should always agree with everyone. There is a time and a place to argue a point, but realistically you only get a small number of those before you become a net negative, so use them wisely. Unless you're a designer, don't lock up over color choices or themes, and once a decision is made, move past it. It may not be the perfect solution, but once it's cast in stone, it's usually time to just move forward and let it go.

Summary

Solving Problems with Context
- **Be aware of factors outside your tasks**
  - **Other people**
  - **Other systems**
  - **Corporate culture**

Really, you could sum this section up as having an awareness that regardless of what you're building, there is a context, which probably includes other people, other systems, and a corporate culture. Successful developers are able to pull back from their day to day grind and seek to understand why they do what they're doing. They also recognize that no team, no company, or system is perfect, and they learn to function well even when they don't completely agree with decisions being made on a larger scale. Make sure you take some time to understand how the work you are doing fits into something larger, and be flexible on the journey. This will go a long ways towards a better career in software.

Module 5 : Brand

Introduction

Taking Care of Your Reputation
- **Guarding the way you are seen**
  - **Personal brand**
  - **The importance of networking**
  - **Being social (as in social media)**
  - **The poison of politics and religion**

Taking care of your reputation. Okay, I can already feel some of you rolling your eyes, and to some extent I get it. When we start talking about managing your reputation, it brings thoughts of image management, shallow people, phoniness, and such. And while that does happen with some people, consider this, you cannot not have a reputation. Everyone that knows you has an opinion about you. Do you want that opinion to be accurate? You see, it's not so much about creating a false front, it's more about letting people see who you really are and what you really do best. In the same way you want your resume to be honest and positive, your reputation is a living, breathing alternative to the formal, written resume. And much like a great resume, a great reputation is central to having a better career in software. With that stated, let's take a look at four aspects of taking care of your reputation, and we'll dive into each of these areas later in this section of the book. Number one is personal brand. This is about making sure your "subtitle" is accurate. Number two is the relevance of networking. This is making the most of your interactions. Number three I've called it being social. What we really mean there is how social media shapes your reputation. And number four, kind of the converse to that, the poison of politics and religion and how that can affect your success.

Personal Brand

Again, I'm sure some of you are rolling your eyes at the idea of managing your brand. There is something about developers that lends itself to letting your coding skills speak for themselves, and that's a noble thing, but it's incomplete. Think about it this way, if you wrote a great software library, one that could help a lot of people, would you just stick it on a file server and hope people stumbled across it? Of course not. You would want to make sure people knew what it could do so it could help them in their work. It's not bragging about the library, it's making sure people know what it has and what it does. And the same thing can be said of your skill set. You have a user interface, if people don't know what you can do, how will they know to hire you? How will they know to request you for their team? How will they know to ask you to speak or write about a topic if they don't know you can do it? Branding is something that may sound flashy and sales-y, but the reality is, you should be able to let people know what you're good at. It's also helpful to ask a few trusted friends, what is your current brand? Ask them what you are best at doing. Do you agree with what they say? If so, great! If not, maybe you need to consider working on your brand. And even more importantly, do you know what your manager really thinks about you? Realistically, this has a direct impact on your short term success. In most cases, managers determine raises, they determine promotions, they pick people for projects, and they even make decisions around layoffs. How would your manager describe your skill set? Is it accurate? If not, you probably need to take some time to work on your brand. In the next few sections we'll talk about specific ways to help you clarify your brand among your peers.

Networking

Often times developers see networking as more brown nosing, because some people abuse the idea in that fashion. It is true that there are people out there who abuse the concept, but don't make the mistake of dismissing networking because some people do that. It is important to communicate what you're doing so people can understand what you bring to the table. And when I talk about networking I'm referring to, for example, attending meetings in person rather than via online, I'm talking about attending lunchtime and after work learning sessions, local user groups, meet-ups, and other live events. Meeting people is key to finding new opportunities in your career. If people don't know who you are or what you do, they're never going to recruit you to work for them. Formal channels like recruiters are helpful, but in the end most of the opportunities I've been involved with came via existing relationships. Unless you are spectacular interviewer, and I know I'm not, you should think heavily about where and how you're connecting with other developers, especially outside your core team. Don't get turned off by the people who abuse it, instead focus on making sure you are connecting with other developers who share your areas of interest. There's also something to be said about learning from the people who you're around. Solomon, who was repeated to be the wisest man that ever lived, once said, he who walks with the wise grows wise, but the companion of fools suffers harm. You will likely learn a lot as you hang out with fellow developers. It's human nature to emulate people you are around, and being with developers, especially those who are interested in growing their careers is a very good thing. Successful developers rarely hide out in their cubes all day, there is a time to go heads down and work, but connecting with other developers is a key component to a better career in software.

Social Media

In addition to meeting people in person, you can do a lot of great networking via social networks. This can range from more traditional exchanges like forums, blogs, and distribution lists, to more recent entries like Twitter and Facebook. For developers, some of the traditional venues, like forums, actually provide a great form of networking. Conversations are often around some technical issue and it involves a question, some time spent investigating, and a response. Many developers I've talked with have said they have no interest in public speaking or book authoring, or that kind of thing, but many of them are deep thinkers and great problems solvers, so I encourage them to go answer two or three questions a month in some technical forum. Over time that creates a stellar reputation and you learn a lot in the process. Some developers do enjoy writing and books are a great way to improve your reputation. To be clear, you don't make much money writing books. That's not why you author them. You author them so that you can point to a shelf and show your expertise in print. But the reality is most of us don't have time to write a book, so social media provides some great alternatives. Twitter is great for pithy sayings, but for a more meaty topic you might consider blogging. Blogging is not for everyone, but if you enjoy it you can build a great reputation over time, and it's not that hard to do. The biggest mistake I see people make with a blog, is they write long detailed posts that effectively empty their knowledge in one fell swoop. I always encourage people to take a topic and break it into 5 or 10 parts as a short series with weekly updates and give away the knowledge in shorter, consumable steps. This can create momentum and allows you to stage your blog posts ahead of time. Of course, if you do the heavier things like blogging in forums, you can use Twitter to link to them and drive traffic. Other developers like doing how-to videos and posting them, or writing code samples and publishing them for others to use. One other thing that you should consider is keeping your online profile current via a service like LinkedIn. Sending around your resume indicates you are actively looking for a new job and that can hurt you in a current situation. However, if you keep your resume updated online, especially via something like LinkedIn, or as a page on your blog, it does not look suspicious at all. Further, I want people to know what I do so they can contact me with appropriate opportunities, not because I'm constantly unhappy in my job, it's just a matter of communicating my skill set. I always encourage developers to find a way that works for them to connect online and use that. There really is something for almost everyone online, including a paradigm to engage that feels most natural. The point is to find a way to connect with your peers so that you can be known, not for a phony front, but for what you actually do well.

Politics and Religion

Amidst all the options for social media and expression, I've seen too many developers take their platform and use it to sabotage their reputation by going political or religious. Let me state up front, there's nothing wrong with having political or religious views, that kind of debate is healthy, but it doesn't have a lot to do with software. And if you mix it in with software, you're going to turn off a bunch of people who believe something different. I've had many situations over the years where I'm mentoring developers and they go out on their blogs and they rant about something political. My advice to them has been to either start up a second blog where they can do political or religious things, or just keep it out of their technical blogs altogether. Most of the recent elections have been close in terms of voting percentages, which generally means you're going to anger half your reader base with any kind of political comment. If you must do something like that, just keep it completely separate from your technical content. This is also true in terms of conversations in person. It's dangerous to assume what someone believes. I would advise keeping political and religious opinions to yourself, at least in the context of your technical branding. Feel free to go crazy with is elsewhere, just recognize that it creates divisions.

Summary

Taking Care of Your Reputation
- **You will be known for something**
    - **Guarding your brand**
    - **Networking**
    - **Social media**
    - **Avoiding political rants**

The bottom line with your reputation is this, perception is reality, at least in the short term. And your brand, your conversations, and your online presence, this is what shapes those perceptions. Successful developers are aware of this and they take steps to make sure their reputation is accurate. Be aware that you will have a reputation and you have the ability to make it represent you well.

Module 6 : Interactions

Introduction

Working and Playing Well with Others
  - **Interacting with people**
    - **Listening before responding**
    - **Taking advice**
    - **Working in a silo**
    - **Basic hygiene**
    - **Doing too much**

The last principle I've included in this book is probably the softest of the soft skills, getting along with other people. I suspect almost everything I say in this section will be something you already know, but having spent so much time with so many developers, and having seen the same issues over and over, I have to mention this. It is arguably the most known, but least practiced of these five principles. And I've tried to break it into some very tangible tactics that can help you incorporate it into your daily routine. These five areas include, number one, listening before responding. Number two, taking advice or criticism. Number three, working in a silo. Number four, basic hygiene. And number five, doing too much. Let's take a deeper look at each of these areas.

Listening

Listening before responding is such a basic human skill. It applies well outside of software development, but it is central to the critical conversations within a software team. As developers we live and die by our data. Information is like gold for us and part of our sense of worth comes from knowing things. So when someone asks us a question, it is in our nature to process the answer while they are still asking, and basically start the answer in our heads well before we've heard the whole question. This can lead to talking past each other and generally poor communication. It may feel unnatural, but if you are asked a direct question, try listening all the way to the end and then repeat the question back to confirm to them you heard it correctly. You would be surprised at how helpful this style of reflective listening is. Not only does it clarify the question and give you a little time to process it, it also validates to the other person that you are listening to them. Think of it as a checksum, we do this in software for reliable communication, so why wouldn't we do it when we're exchanging information about the project? Not with every detail perhaps, but at least for critical questions about the system. If you don't get anything else from this book, just this one thing might be a huge benefit for your team.

Taking Advice

This next item is pretty difficult to hear. Like most of the tactics around the larger principle of working and playing well with others, this is applicable in all areas of your life. To set this one up, let's consider a couple of general truths followed by a question. One, you're not perfect, there are likely a few things you need to change and you may not realize what all of them are. Two, there will be situations where someone points it out to you. Three, they are likely going to have a terribly delivery when they tell you, for a variety of reasons. I won't go into them, but it is human nature that we deliver criticism poorly. Four, it's also human nature to receive criticism poorly, which is where this principle can be a huge point of learning. The question is, how do you receive criticism, especially when it's poorly delivered? It's easy to argue and defend, and in some cases you probably should do that, but at the same time are you big enough to think about what is being said to see if there's any truth in it? Few people are ever just flat out 100% wrong about something. When someone offers you advice, council, or even criticism, there is likely something in there that you ought to heed. As analytical people, we are very good at deflecting criticism and arguing it away. As part of being a more successful developer, I would challenge you to go back, move beyond any poor delivery, and think through whether there is something you can learn from what was said. One of my favorite speakers, Andy Stanley, says this is even harder for leaders at a company because they have the power to brow beat any critics that work for them. He says leaders who don't listen will soon be surrounded by people with nothing to say. That's actually true at all levels and if you make it miserable for someone to offer you any council, you're only hurting yourself in the long run. Successful developers find a way to improve themselves with the criticism they hear, regardless of how badly it is delivered to them.

Silos

The next area to discuss is working in a silo. This is complimentary to the earlier discussion on solving problems in context, but the focus here is on connecting with teammates. Arguably I could have just called this item being agile, as so much of the Agile movement is around having better conversations along the way. The point of those daily stand-ups and various Agile practices is to get conversations going. One of the worst things you can do as a developer is get your specs, disappear into a hole for three months, and emerge with a finished application. That's back for the customer who often doesn't know what they want until they see it. It's bad for other developers who need to interact with you along the way. It's bad for project managers who need a timeline, testers who need to see what they need to test, and architects who are trying to fit all this stuff together. It's hard on everybody who needs to be connected as the project evolves. I won't turn this into a crusade for Agile, I will simply say that successful developers rarely work in isolation and you should look for ways to interact regularly as you build solutions.

Hygiene

Okay, now for the most uncomfortable item on the list, I would rather not even bring it up, but it is something that does happen, and if you have an issue here, trust me, everybody around you already knows it. As a developer, you should be interacting with other people along the way, and this means keeping yourself reasonably clean and presentable. I'm not talking about walking around in a suit and tie, or even dressing in any way above and beyond your company's standard dress code. Rather, what I'm talking about is this, there are some developers who, for lack of a better way to say it, simply don't shower enough, or they wear the same clothes for several days without changing, or they wear offensive clothes, or they have piercings and tattoos that are way beyond the social norm. Now, I'm not condemning any of that, you're free to do and wear whatever you want, but there is a reality, and that is the further you take yourself outside of the social norms of business attire, fashion, and hygiene, the more challenging you will find it to be successful in software. That's simply a reality of our industry.

Doing too Much

One last area for us to cover with working and playing well with others, is doing too much. I like how Confucius said it, a man who chases two rabbits catches none. The idea of focus may seem a bit out of place in the list for working and playing well with others, but I put it here because it manifests in your interactions with other. When you try to do too much, you end up letting things fall off without finishing them, and that shows up as an inability to follow through or execute, and your coworkers will feel that directly. You do not want to develop a reputation as someone who can't get things done. You'll find much more success at doing few things well than trying to do too many things and losing sight of some of them along the way. I also put this in this section because sometimes it originates from an inability to tell somebody no. Often developers are given a full workload, and then they get handed bugs to fix, or little changes to make without any concession for how it impacts their schedule. You have to be willing to tell people no, or at least caveat requests with a time extension to cover the additional effort. Successful developers are able to manage their task list and are strong enough to push back on unrealistic workloads without becoming shrill or unprofessional. You need to guard your workload because it ultimately becomes the loudest statement of your reputation. If you allow quality to suffer, no one will remember in two years that you were overscheduled when you built something. They'll simply remember that it was poorly built, and it was poorly built by you. Guard your workload and you'll find much more success as a developer.

Summary

- Becoming an expertise expert
- Managing your career
- Solving problems in context
- Taking care of your reputation
- Working and playing well with others

In summary, we've looked at five key principles that seem to be common among most successful software developers. We've dipped into a handful of tactics for each principle, hopefully giving you some specific ways to get started in each area. Some of these may feel more applicable than others, and that's fine. No two humans are exactly alike and you'll find certain items more palatable then others. As I've said, this is not intended to be an exhaustive list, but rather a set of common patterns I've seen in the years in the industry. I hope you find value in them.

www.ingramcontent.com/pod-product-compliance
Lightning Source LLC
Chambersburg PA
CBHW070903070326
40690CB00009B/1969